Anonymous

The Art Student in Paris

.

Anonymous

The Art Student in Paris

ISBN/EAN: 9783337429027

Printed in Europe, USA, Canada, Australia, Japan

Cover: Foto ©Thomas Meinert / pixelio.de

More available books at **www.hansebooks.com**

IN PARIS.

i

PUBLISHED BY THE
BOSTON ART STUDENTS' ASSOCIATION.
1887.

CONTENTS.

INTRODUCTION.

THIS little book is the outcome of a meeting of the Art Students' Association, held during the past winter, when several letters were read by older members, who had studied in Paris, in which they related their impressions of the life and schools, and offered suggestions drawn from their own experience to younger members who are looking forward to a similar course of study. Enough questions are asked, and enough interest is shown in this matter, outside the Association, to warrant these members in addressing themselves to a larger audience.

To every young American, studying Art, a stay in Europe is an expectation or a dream of the future; yet many are able to give so short a time to study or travel, that it is extremely important their preparation should be in the right direction.

We are well aware that individual circumstances will differ, and we have therefore tried to state the experiences of several students, to picture the conditions of French Studios — both for men and women — the splendid opportunities easily attained by the former, and the restricted ones that are conceded to the latter, the severity of professors, the intense competition, the ardor of work, the bad air, the noise and confusion, the delights, dangers and disillusions, that await every young aspirant in a Parisian School of Art. We have tried to show that Paris — though it may aid one in practicing small economies — is not an easy place to live in on "nothing certain a year"; for, hard work, combined with rigid economy through a disagreeable Parisian winter, may undermine a strong constitution, and produce disastrous effects in after-life.

To those who have aided us with good advice and practical suggestions, we own ourselves greatly indebted, and we trust our readers will have as lively an experience of gratitude.

It has been our endeavor, as far as possible, to give the addresses of schools, names of professors, and fees, correctly, for this year; but as nothing, even in Europe, is permanent, we must be pardoned if some changes occur. The addresses of Pensions have been given by those residing in Paris as Art students; but, in the matter of boarding-houses, even the best friends are apt to disagree. We give them, as recommended to us, for their convenience, comfort, and (for Paris) low rate of board.

For the young men and women in whose interest this little work is published — those who are obliged to count the months and days of their stay in Paris, and are, therefore, glad to profit by the experience of others — we trust that our labor will be a help and an enlightenment.

I

THE NECESSITY OF PREPARATORY STUDY.

THERE has been so general an interest of late in the History of Art, and so many people are able to recite a correct list of the Madonnas of Raphael, or to name the museums containing the principal works of Rembrandt, without realizing the great difference between them, that artists are sometimes led into the opposite error of regarding all such information as desirable only for wealthy tourists or the enslaved disciples of Ruskin.

Though a knowledge of the lives of artists — their temperament — the people among whom they lived and the events of contemporaneous history does not in itself make men paint better, it does help in the comprehension and enjoyment of the master works. It kindles enthusiasm for the profession they have chosen, and makes it nobler and worthier. *History of Art helps the Student.*

The best art has so close a relation to the age that produced it that it can be understood only through history. If Veronese and Jan Steen had changed countries, who can tell what the refined splendor of Venetian life would have *Influence of the Age and Surroundings on the Artist.*

done for the one, or how the grosser pleasures of Holland would have transformed the other. The best museums — the Louvre for instance — display their treasures grouped in the different National Schools of Art; yet, even with this aid, an ignorant person will find them bewildering.

A student trained in the modern realistic school of out-of-door painting, where mystery and gloom are never seen, where the main effort is to reproduce or cleverly suggest well known facts of nature, will find these leagues of embrowned canvases full of strange, unreal visions, decidedly perplexing.

The Old Masters Difficult for the Modern Student to understand.
They will, doubtless, admire the good drawing so beautiful and unconscious, the fine modelling, the power and elegance displayed in portraiture, but they will confess it easier for them to get a good lesson from some modern work — by Lerolle or Carolus Duran for instance — where the intention is easily understood, and the effort to paint well distinctly visible. One reason of this perplexity is that the aims of art differ in various eras, and with different men. In order to profit truly by their works, it is necessary to sympathize with them, to try to understand their endeavors and to have a knowledge of the incentives and obstacles that beset them. Such information certainly prepares the mind to receive much deeper impressions, even of the technical ability they display.

According to their view, to paint a picture was not to select a bit of nature haphazard, but to compose it agreeably as regarded movement of figures, masses of light and shade,

and disposition of color. As a result their fine compositions
become a delight to the eye before one
has a clear conception of the subject.
Corot — the poet and idol of landscape
painters — once said: "I try to paint Nature as the good
God has made it, and a little like Claude Lorraine." The
beautiful composition of Claude, his wonderful gradation of
light, could not but impress an eye as sensitive as Corot's.
A landscape of Poussin's, that hangs in the Salon Carré, is
so finely disposed on the canvas, that at a distance it has a
decorative effect like superb tapestry. These men — Claude
and Poussin — echoed the sentiments of another age, when
classic elegance had supreme sway: but, to an educated
mind, what teachers they become! They help a student,
though he may be in sympathy with his own age, and its less
studied tastes, to greater refinement and a love of the beautiful. One could easily tell, from the pictures of Millet and
Bastien LePage, that they knew the French peasant, by close
contact; but, does it not help, rather than hinder, an appreciation of their art to know of the realities and struggles of
their lives? They, and the Knights of Labor, are products
of our own time, just as Fragonard and Boucher, the fetes
champêtres and the pretty unreal dairies of Versailles are
of another.

It seems as if an artist would instinctively crave information of this sort; but, it is so easy, amid the absorbing
problems that beset every one in attaining the alphabet of
art, to forget that anything is necessary but ability to repro-

(margin note) Ideas of the Old Masters in Landscape Composition.

duce or suggest certain visible facts. The student who has **Neglect of Proper** a limited time to study in Europe, will **Study of Old Pictures.** find in the excitement and competition of foreign schools, in the strange, brilliant life about him, so much to occupy his mind, that the valuable lessons he may receive from old pictures can easily be overlooked. Especially will it be the case, if he is ignorant of the great schools of art, and their distinguishing traits. A visit to the Louvre will seem to him a much less direct, and therefore less desirable way of attaining what he is after, and he will find in modern art a language easily understood and quite within his range.´ Every time he visits the Louvre he is called upon to make a mental effort for which he has neither the time nor the strength, and he will end in taking a great deal of his artistic information at second hand. As we said before, the study of the history of art may not make a man any better as a painter, but, by making him more intelligent, he will be a more perceptive student, and therefore a better artist.

Opinions differ widely as to whether the student should **Preparatory Study in** spend much time in working in the schools **American Schools.** here, preparatory to going to Europe. Some eminent artists think that a long and severe training at home is necessary for a full appreciation of the advantages of foreign schools, while others advocate going to Paris as soon as possible. In our estimation it depends largely on the length of the time the student is able to remain. If he can give but a year or two to his foreign study, then let him first have thorough preparation in the schools here, which are of acknowledged excellence. Although he may have a few things to unlearn, he will be able to turn his limited time to far greater profit in every way. However, if he is so fortunate as to have an indefinite number of years before him which he can devote to the study of art in its very home, then let us advise him not to lose a moment, but to go at once. The most serious objection to a number of years' residence in a foreign country is that it invariably unfits a man or woman to live at home afterwards. Whether this is an advantage or disadvantage, from an artistic point of view, can hardly be discussed here.

The student cannot give too much attention to the language of the country in which he means to study. And although he will learn to **Language.** speak the language much faster in the land where it is universally spoken, he will be saved much time and many discomforts and embarrassments if he can at least read understandingly before leaving home.

This is of the highest importance not only in all matters of travelling and daily life, but in order to be treated as an equal and a comrade in the school. The Parisian student will not be bored by listening to a hesitating utterance, or with repeating his own remarks a second time to accommodate an imperfect comprehension. This necessary command of language is only gained by constant observation, not only of French, but studio French. Without it the student cannot comprehend the instruction of the master, who having himself learned to think and talk of art in the same atmosphere, uses terms, expressions, words with special meaning, often greatly at variance with their usual sense, delicate shades, difficult to explain, impossible to translate, which grow up, no doubt, in all languages where art is talked of; full of intelligence to the elect, jargon to the Philistine.

Thus many important points are lost to the student who has only book French, and still more to the unfortunate who depends on a bystander to translate the directions of the professor — a favor nearly all must ask at first — even if the translator does not yield to a good natured temptation to soften the harsh words of criticism, falling so easily from the lips of a European master.

The pride of his local art school, will not always believe that even a member of the Institute Français can think so meanly of his work as his neighbor has stated. Very bitter feeling has often been engendered by a most softened rendering — with the omission of many harrowing details — of the advice not to paint a full figure, but to draw a foot or hand from the cast, because the *nouveau* knows so little and that little is so mistaken.

II.

STUDIO LIFE.

O N arriving in Paris the student is apt to be confused by
the number of opportunities offer-
ed. It is only after visiting the different   Selection of Atelier.
studios, or even after a month's residence, that he is able
to decide which is the most likely to meet his particular
needs.

After selecting his atelier he should resign his will to the
direction of his master while he remains
in the school. If he dislikes the methods   Conduct.
there taught, let him change for another, always remembering
that everywhere there will be some cause of dissatisfaction.
Intelligent obedience is the only road to a master's interest
and attention. If the student shows a disposition to set up
his own judgment in opposition to his master's advice, he is
very likely to be left to get on as he can. By this an imitation of the personal methods and mannerisms of the master
is not meant, neither is it wished nor encouraged : it would
be impossible, where, as in most schools, two professors come
alternately, and are painters of widely differing ages, styles
and views. The student should remember that the professor

has seen the work of hundreds of other students, that at the beginning all are alike interesting, and at the same time, indifferent to him ; that his advice, however unpalatable, is the result of honest conviction founded on long experience and wide knowledge. Very little notice is taken by the professors of mediocre work, whereas if a pupil shows extraordinary ability, they give him considerable personal attention. Instead of helping the weaker pupils to raise themselves to the standard of the others, all attention is given to those who show ability, and the better the student works, the more help he receives from his teacher. He will not, however, always receive the most benefit from the instruction of the painter whose work he most admires, nor should he slight the suggestions of a teacher because he does not like his pictures.

The hours in most of the studios are from 8 A. M. to 12 M., and from 1 P. M. to 5 P. M., or until **Hours.** dark during the short days of winter. At "Julien's" there is a class without instruction in the evening. Time will not be gained in the end by trying to make the school day too long. Most ateliers are packed full of students and are quite unventilated and overheated. The air is bad beyond description. If the student does his best during the four morning hours (and the visits of the professors are in the morning), he will accomplish more in the year than if he stays fatigued and benumbed by the heat throughout the entire day and evening, unless he is gifted with unusual health and strength. Even then he can use the short winter afternoons to better advantage in the galleries and exhibi-

tions of Paris. He must learn to work not only in bad air but in a constant noise and confusion.
Noise and Confusion.
Loud talk, argument, harangue, singing, whistling, imitations of the opera, the concerts from the Chateau d'Eau to the Café Chantant, the commands and trumpet calls of the review, the cries of the animals of the Jardin des Plantes, and of unknown beasts, sometimes a tone picture called " Napoleon en Egypt," adding imitation volleys of musketry and boom of cannon and shouts of " Vive l'Empereur" to the usual uproar, last through working hours and rests with but occasional lulls, except during the visit of the professor, when the most profoundly respectful stillness reigns, save for the low murmur of his remarks as he goes quietly from easel to easel. At the end of the lesson all rise and bow in answer to his "Au revoir, Messieurs." When the door is closed behind him, and the sound of his footsteps dies away in the antechamber, the tempest wakes again. At first this is very distracting, but one soon becomes so habituated to it, that the confusion seems as necessary and as proper an accompaniment to earnest school work as drums and fifes to a hard march.

The ateliers for women are calm and quiet compared with those for the men, but there is also enough noise to be at first very bewildering. The
Ateliers for Women.
first time we went into the women's class at the Atelier Julien, which is perhaps the most crowded and popular in Paris, it seemed impossible that any one ever could accomplish any serious work there, the air was so close and the

heat so intense. It is situated in a crowded part of the city on a gallery of the Passage des Panoramas, the last place we expected to find it. Although it is considered unhealthy, any moderately strong woman may work there without running much risk if she takes plenty of out of door exercise and sleep. At eight o'clock in the morning the model poses, and the girls begin to arrive, and by half past eight all are hard at work. It is the exception for a student to be later than nine o'clock. At twelve comes the noon rest of an hour, and then there is a general rush for the restaurants, though some stay in the atelier and take their lunch there — a practice not to be approved of. At one o'clock many of the students go back to the atelier again, though quite as many go away, perhaps to their own studios, if they have them, or to some other classes, but generally to some kind of work. The model poses from two until five, and after three o'clock there is a class in modelling, and once a week a lecture on anatomy. On Saturday morning the master comes, and his entrance inspires the same awe and is followed by the same stillness as in the men's atelier.

In most ateliers a subject for composition is given out

Composition. on Saturday, the sketches to be made during the week, usually from well known stories of Sacred History, Plutarch, Homer or Virgil, and submitted for the judgment of the professor the following Saturday. The most interesting moments of the day are when the professor stands before the collected sketches, the students crowded thickly about him, looking over each other's shoulders, listening with breathless interest to his running comment, censure, qualified praise, ridicule, suggestion and advice. The professor inquires for the author of each sketch in turn before examining it, and makes his remarks and questions a personal dialogue with the artist, sometimes ending with a little impromptu lecture suggested by the work before him.

There are special courses in anatomy at the Beaux Arts every Sunday morning, to which women are admitted, where the instruction is most admirable and more thorough than in the schools. **Anatomy.**

It is hardly known here among those inexperienced in Parisian life, how universal the custom is for students as well as those who are already established as artists, to exhibit in the Salon. During the months of January and February the attendance in the large ateliers is apt to diminish, as the time is given to the Salon picture, which, as we all know, does not mean necessarily a picture that has been exhibited in the Salon. It is only one which may be, and which very often is not. These attempts are almost always submitted to the inspection of the professor before they are sent in for the final decision of the jury, and the unfailing interest and kindly criticism with which he receives them is a great encouragement and incentive. Of course, in Paris the student is influenced quite as much by the pictures and things he sees, as he is by the work done in the schools, or the corrections from the masters. The inestimable value of having free access **The Salon.**

---

to the great galleries should be well understood and made the most of.

Another important advantage to be gained by European **Companionship.** study, too often entirely neglected, is the cultivation of the acquaintance of Europeans, particularly painters and art students. Painting, more than other arts, is lacking in written record. The processes and science are largely matters of oral tradition, handed down by painters from generation to generation, and rarely finding their way into print. Few painters, like Da Vinci, Reynolds, and Fromentin have been authors. Most of the vast accumulation of " Art Literature " is the work of those who, however learned about painters and pictures, knew little and cared less about painting for its own sake, or painted badly. Where painters, real live painters are to be found, the air is thick with useful suggestion and practical information, the results of personal experiment and tradition. In the art centres of the old world, the traditions of centuries of endeavor are enshrined in the memories of unnumbered painters, each holding his little fragment of the great structure, his part of the wisdom of the ages, sometimes a foundation on which he will build a noble work of art, sometimes a hammer of Thor, all powerful in the strong hand, though his be too weak to lift it. In either case, it is a lesson to be imparted, and only to be learned in the free interchange of studio talk.

Painters, who like poor, sordid Turner, have made a secret of their work — as if a picture were a patent pill — have been

rare indeed, and their secrets little worth knowing. The
normal painter is like Chaucer's clerk :

" And gladly wolde he lerne, and gladly teche."

The teachers with whom the student has worked in America
have given him a part of this great heri-   Advantage of Inter-
tage. The professor in Paris, Munich or   course with Foreign
wherever he goes in Europe, adds many   Students.
new ideas, but the time and attention of the professor must
be divided among so many, the lesson is so short, the respect inspired by the great man is of so awful a nature, that
many a question he would gladly answer is unasked. Thus
the instruction of the master is a less important factor in the
great good to be got from a course of study in Europe than
the influence of the other students more experienced or
naturally stronger than the *nouveau.*

As a rule, men in Europe enter art schools younger and
remain longer than in America, and stay   Benefit of a Compan-
under the master's care after painting   ion in the Galleries.
pictures that would justify a young American at home in
setting up a studio and receiving pupils of his own. Not
only in learning to paint in the studio, but in studying the
works of the masters in the galleries, is the companionship
equally valuable of those who have learned by long association with pictures how to look at them and what to look for.
Seeing — no less than painting — pictures is an art, a faculty
susceptible of cultivation and infinite extension and refine-

ment. Though it is best to go often alone to the galleries and devote the mind to an uninterrupted communion with the thought of the masters in their work, when one goes with a companion, if he is well chosen, a thousand points will be observed, beauties enjoyed, and ideas received that the solitary student would be years in discovering.

The great number of Americans cut themselves off from **Clannishness of Americans in Paris.** the inestimable benefit of this companionship. Starting for France with a very imperfect acquaintance with the language, the American is confident of getting on well, because "there are so many Americans in Paris." No one who has experienced it can recall without gratitude or overestimate the help and generous kindness of Americans already established to the new men, in all the trouble of getting settled and learning the details of a life so different in every respect from our own. The *nouveau* finds his compatriots and the British contingent so agreeable, he looks for no other companions. He selects the school where he will find the greatest number of Americans. During the rests he chats only with the English-speaking, eats only at restaurants frequented by them, spends his evenings in their rooms, at the cafés where they congregate, or if he has a taste for society, at receptions in the American Colony. So far as personal intercourse goes, he might as well be in America. Of course he has the feast of the best art, old and new, the unspoken influence of work better than his own, always before his eyes, if he will use them.

The French student and Latin Quarter painter is often a wild, unkempt youth of rather formidable appearance. His manners are neither nice nor wise. His grand object in life — after the Prix de Rome — is to escape being bored. In spite of his truculent *blague* — Thackeray cleverly translates *blague* as "*French* humbug as distinguished from all other kinds of humbug" — his wild necktie, his bangs, his pose as a terrible fellow, gay, reckless of everything, disrespectful to everyone — but his master, always on the alert to amuse, no matter how, he is, ninety-nine cases out of a hundred, like artists everywhere, an exceedingly good fellow, often with curious funds of unexpected learning, perfectly frank to admire and praise anything appealing to him as strong, and free from the false sense of politeness which keeps one painter from calling the attention of a comrade to the faults and weakness of the latter's work. No one who has ever enjoyed this stimulating society, will forget the gratuitous lessons received from fellow students, men young and little known.

The French Art Student.

Mr. Hunt walking on the plain of Barbizon with Jean François Millet, drinking in the influence we all feel so strongly to-day, is a shining example of the high possibilities of this international companionship. It is not given to us to walk with Millet or look upon his like, but the benefit of such intercourse will be shared in a greater or less degree by all who seek it.

Influence of Millet on Hunt.

The American must not make the mistake of thinking, that to get on well with the Frenchmen he must imitate their tricks

and their manners. The more intelligent French students
have the perception rare with us — that the manners of
Aping French   each nation are the logical result of the
Manners.   nation's habits and natural character ;
each good in its own way, and far better than an imitation
of the forms of any other people. The *distinction français*
is one thing, and the *distinction anglais* is quite another.
Then they wish to have the stage to themselves and like the
foreigner best as an amused spectator. No foreigner —
except a suspected Prussian — is so unpopular as an American who attempts to imitate, which the English never do,
their shocking antics.

In the summer, when he leaves the schools for some grey-
                        walled village in the fields or by the sea,
Vacation.   let the student keep his interest in the
people as people, not as mere models. If he will play with
the children at dusk, talk with the women in the fields, the
men in the shops and at the *auberge*, see the village *fête*, and
listen to the *grand'mère* in her chimney corner, he will learn
to care for them, and paint them as pictures of life, not mere
studies of blue jean and sabots with figures inside, and will
lay up stores of pleasant memories ; for all will agree, in the
end, it is not the great spectacles of the world that are
remembered most vividly and pleasantly when old times are
recalled — and times grow old so soon ! An old woman
spinning by her lamp, a white-capped baby on the grass, or a
trail of ivy on the wall, is more to us than the Grand Opera
or the towers of Notre Dame.

III.

EXPENSE AND MODE OF LIVING.

IT is almost as hard to decide how and where to live in Paris as it is to know where to study. All degrees of luxury or discomfort are **Cost of Living.** open to the student according to the extent of his letter of credit. It is naturally much easier for a man to find a cheap convenient mode of living than a woman, though her limitations in the matter are not as great as are usually supposed. But there is one point which must be recognized from the beginning — that in almost every case it costs a woman much more to live in Paris than a man. At some of the most desirable ateliers the fees are double those of the men, and where there are twenty cheap restaurants that men can go to, there is but one for women. In various other ways her expenses are increased, so that she should never plan to spend a winter there on some of the low estimates of expenditures given by men. Increase them by one-third and she will find she has to exercise the strictest economy to keep within her allowance. It is very difficult to determine the exact cost of a winter, as every one differs, and it is so much easier for some people than for others, to economize. One member of our Association, a man who had two winters' experience in the great city, writes : — "The life is a pleasant and inexpensive one, and one soon learns how to live in the most inexpensive manner. One can have comfortable apartments, eat good food, pay tuition fees at the studio and buy all necessary materials for five hundred dollars a year. Very many students live on less than that, but I am telling of my experience the first year I was in Paris. In the country places which the students frequent, one can live for the same sum and even less." This, let us remark, is rather an extreme view. It may be done, for it has been done, but we caution the student not to attempt it, unless he has vigorous health and a strong constitution. We venture to suggest that from $800 to $1,000 for a man, and from $1,000 to $1,200 for a woman is a comfortable allowance for a year; it always costs more than the ambitious economist thinks it will, though as experience comes, the francs disappear less rapidly, and the savings of the second winter may cover the extra expenditure of the first. It seems a pity that in making these suggestions, we cannot go further and tell how to avoid any unnecessary outlay; but some things can be learned only through personal experience, and this is among them.

The different ways of living might be classed under four heads.

Mode of Living.

1. Hotels.
2. Boarding-houses or "Pensions."
3. Apartments or studios.
4. Single rooms.

The larger hotels are given in the Baedeker's Guide, and they, or the life in them hardly need be
mentioned here. Comfortable board and **Hotels.**
rooms may be found in some of the small hotels for seven ($1.40) and eight ($1.60) francs a day and even less ; and a room (high up, to be sure, but all rooms seem high up in Paris) alone, costs about two francs (40 cents) a day. In this case the "first breakfast" is taken in some convenient " Creamery " on the way to the studio, for twenty-five to fifty centimes (5 to 10 cents), and the more substantial meals at a restaurant for a franc and a quarter to three francs, or 25 to 60 cents.

The boarding-houses or "pensions" vary in price according to locality. The cheaper ones are from **Boarding Houses or**
six ($1.20) to ten francs ($2.00) a day. **Pensions.**
This way of living is not as independent as the other, though it is often more convenient, especially for a woman alone, and affords material help in learning the language.

If two or three women wish to live together, a small apartment can be found for a very low price in **Apartments or**
some of the unfashionable quarters of the **Studios.**
city, such as that around the Place Ternes, the Clichy quarter, or around the Luxembourg Gardens. Or they can find a studio with a room or two attached for seventy-five ($15.00) to one hundred francs ($20.00) a month. The furniture need be of the simplest description, and is found in the second hand stores for very little money, though for beds we should recommend the " Bon Marché." Housekeeping is made easy

by hiring the concierge to do the " chores," getting one's own breakfast of the regulation chocolate and bread, and either going to a restaurant for the other meals or having them sent in. This last system is not nearly as expensive as is imagined, and after a short time the minimum of portions for the maximum of partakers is easily reached.

Separate rooms are the most easy to find, as there are large houses where furnished rooms can **Rooms.** be had for a very small cost. The manner of living would be about the same as in the apartments, and the expense probably less.

Of course in Paris, as in other great cities, prices are much lower in some quarters than in others. **Location.** It may be stated generally, that the left bank of the Seine is rather cheaper than the right, though Montmartre rivals the Latin Quarter in its marvels of economy. In choosing the location of one's abode, preference should be given to the higher land about the Luxembourg Gardens and the Pantheon, and on the other side of the river, on the unfashionable side of the Arc de Triomphe ; the Ternes, for example, and the Boulevards Courcelles. The dark, narrow streets of the Latin Quarter, such as the Rue de Bac and Rue Jacob, should be avoided in spite of their interesting surroundings, as they are damp and extremely unhealthy. A student may live there after he has become thoroughly acclimated, but if he goes there at first he runs great risk of getting typhoid fever, which is well known to be the scourge of Paris.

The climate of Paris is raw and chilly in winter, though the thermometer seldom falls below 25° **Climate.** Fahr. The dampness is so penetrating, that it is much harder to keep warm than in our colder and more variable climate. However, this weather lasts but a short time — during December and January principally — and the rest of the year it is even and pleasant.

To conclude, let us try to dispel an illusion which has blinded many of our fellow students, and **Mistaken Ideas of** which only bitter experience has proved **the Cost of Living.** to be false. In spite of the low estimates of expenditure already given in these pages, it is a fallacy that one can live in Paris on less than one can here. The actual cost of things is as great, except in a few instances, and the only reason it is done is because people go without things that they would consider actually necessary on this side of the ocean, put up with all kinds of inconveniences, and endure cold and even hunger for the sake of living as cheaply as possible. The fact is true, however, that we get more enjoyment out of money there than here, for the very reason that we are not obliged by circumstances to spend it on things we do not actually need.

IV.

SCHOOLS.

THE academies and ateliers here given are those best known and most frequented by Americans in Paris. In the Academies Julien, Champs Elysées, Merson, Colarossi and Krug, a nude model poses the whole or half the day, and the expense of models is included in the fees. At most of the other studios, students pay for the models. The Champs Elysées is the only academy where women have two regular criticisms a week as is customary in the men's classes. In many academies the fees for women are much larger than those demanded from men, the reason being that many of the students are not studying professionally, and consequently instruction as a luxury is put at a higher price. The work done in the women's schools is much inferior to the men's, though in the schools for men and women, the latter have opportunities from time to time of seeing the former's work.

Large Schools.

ECOLE DES BEAUX ARTS.

The examinations for admission to the Beaux Arts occur twice a year, in February and July. They consist of examinations in History, Perspective, Anatomy, Architecture, Drawing, and Modeling. The first three are called the "Concours de place." The pupils who do not reach a certain standard in these are dropped. Those having the highest marks are given the first choice of place in drawing from the model.

For the examination in History, a list of questions is prepared, which can be obtained from the Secretary of the School about a month before the examination takes place. This list consists of about thirty-five questions. At the examinations two of these questions are given, and the pupil has the choice of answering one or both of them. The answers can be written in English if one prefers.

In Perspective some simple problem is given.

In Anatomy a drawing of one or two of the bones of the human body is required; such as the fore-arm and elbow, or the femur and the knee joint.

In Architecture the pupil is required to draw to scale a simple column or entablature of one of the five orders. The drawing occupies a week, two hours each day, making twelve in all. As the names are called, each one takes his place, the names being arranged according to the standing in the "Concours de place." The drawings are generally made on charcoal paper, with charcoal, as is common in the schools. In the winter the drawings are usually made from the living model; in summer from the cast.

For the examination in Modeling, one is expected to copy in clay a bas-relief head from the antique.

The examinations occupy about a month, and when many

apply several divisions are made. This gives frequently two or three days between the examinations, which is a great advantage for preparatory study. Those who pass the examinations have the privilege of studying in one of the ateliers, of attending lectures and other advantages of the school for two years, free of expense.

One is expected to pay a small fee in entering the atelier for the use of easels and stools; also to treat or pay "punch" as it is called.

One can usually find American students at the Beaux Arts, who can furnish the latest information regarding the examinations. The professors of painting at the Beaux Arts are, Gérôme, Cabanel, and Boulanger. On entering the school, the student can choose the professor he prefers and enter his atelier. The professors visit their respective ateliers twice a week, generally Wednesdays and Fridays. The school hours are from 8 to 12.30 in winter, and from 7 to 11.30 in summer. The student generally draws from the model till the professor thinks him sufficiently advanced to take up painting. Those painting and drawing, work together from the same model.

Each student is criticised separately, and individuality is encouraged. Composition is not compulsory, though the professors strongly urge all the students to do as much of it as possible, and are always ready to criticise their sketches. The lectures in Anatomy by Prof. Duval are largely attended by students outside, as well as by those in the Beaux Arts. These lectures take place twice a week and are finely illustrated.

The students spend their afternoons in various ways, some drawing from the antique, others copying in the Louvre or Luxembourg, still others in attending lectures or studying some subject relating to their work. There are two or three ateliers for sculptors, one of them being under the charge of M. Falguiere. It is hardly necessary to say that women are not admitted to the Beaux Arts.

ACADEMIE JULIEN.
FOR MEN.
48 Rue du Faubourg St. Denis, opposite Rue D'Enghien.

PROFESSORS.
Boulanger, Lefebvre, Tony Robert Fleury, Bouguereau.

FEES.
For One Month.

Mornings, 8 to 12, ...	Twenty-five Francs.
Afternoons, 1 to 5, ...	Thirty Francs.
Whole day, ...	Fifty Francs.

For Three Months.

Whole day, . .	One hundred and twenty-five Francs.

For Six Months.

Whole day, ...	Two hundred Francs.

For One Year.

Whole day, ...	Three hundred Francs.

A Prize of one hundred francs is awarded every month.

FOR WOMEN.

Passage des Panoramas, 27 Galerie Montmartre.

PROFESSORS.

Boulanger, Lefebvre, Tony Robert Fleury.

FEES.

For One Month.

Half day, ...	Sixty Francs.
Whole day, ...	One hundred Francs.

For Three Months.

Half day, ...	One hundred Francs.
Whole day, .	Two hundred and fifty Francs.

For Six Months.

Half day, . .	Two hundred and fifty Francs.
Whole day, . .	Four hundred Francs.

For One Year.

Half day, ...	Four hundred Francs.
Whole day, ...	Seven hundred Francs.

There are no vacations in the Academie Julien.

ACADEMIE COLAROSSI.

STUDIOS FOR MEN AND WOMEN.

8 Rue de la Grande Chaumière ; also 39 Avenue d'Eylau or Victor Hugo.

PROFESSORS.

Colin, Courtois, Dagnan-Bouveret, Hiolle, Pousans, Schutzenberger.

FEES.

FOR MEN AND WOMEN.

39 Avenue d'Eylau.

One week, ... Fifteen Francs.

For One Month.

Half day, ... Forty Francs.
Whole day, ... Sixty Francs.

For Three Months.

Half day, ... One hundred and five Francs.

For Ten Months (year).

Half day, ... Two hundred and fifty Francs.
Whole day, . . . Four hundred Francs.

FOR MEN.

For One Month.

Half day,   .   .   . Twenty-five Francs.

Rue de la Grande Chaumière.

FEES.

FOR MEN.

For One Month.

Day, ... Sixteen Francs.

Evening, ... Fifteen Francs.

FOR WOMEN.

For One Month.

Day, ... Twenty Francs.

Evening, ... Twenty Francs.

An entrance fee of six francs includes easels and stool.

CAROLUS DURAN.

FOR MEN.

88 Boulevard de Port Royal.

PROFESSSOR.

Carolus Duran.

FEES.

One month,	. . . . .	Thirty Francs.
Half year, .	One hundred and twenty-five Francs.	
Year, .	. .	Two hundred Francs.
Entrance fee,	. .	Twenty-five Francs.

FOR WOMEN.

17 Quai Voltaire.

PROFESSORS.

Carolus Duran and Henner.

FEES.

For One Month.

Mornings only,	.	One hundred Francs.
Entrance fee,	. . . .	Ten Francs.

ALFRED STEVENS.

FOR WOMEN ONLY.

No. 16 Avenue Frochot, near Place Pigalle.

FEES.

One month,	. . . .	One hundred Francs.

Daily criticisms.

ATELIER HENRY MOSLER.
28 Faubourg St. Honoré.

MIXED CLASS WITH DRAPED MODEL.

FEES.

For One Month.

Half day, ... Sixty Francs.
Number limited.

EDOUARD KRUG.
FOR WOMEN.
11 Boulevard de Clichy.

PROFESSORS.

Ed. Krug, Feyen-Perrin.

FEES.

For One Month.

Half day, ... Sixty Francs.
Whole day, ... One hundred Francs.

For Three Months.

Whole day, ... Two hundred and fifty Francs.

For Six Months.

Whole day, ... Four hundred Francs.

For One Year.

Whole day, ... Six hundred Francs.

BENJAMIN CONSTANT. VILLA DES ARTS.

15 Impasse Hélène, Avenue Clichy.

FEES.

FOR MEN.

For Three Months.

Half day, ... Seventy Francs.
Whole day, . One hundred and twenty-five Francs.

For Six Months.

Whole day, . Two hundred Francs.

FOR WOMEN.

For One Month.

Half day, . Sixty Francs.

SCHOOL OF DRAWING AND PAINTING.

85 Rue Ampère.

PROFESSORS.

Puvis de Chavannes, Bonnat, Roll.

FEES.

For One Month.

Half day, . . . Sixty Francs.
Whole day, . . One hundred Francs.

Number of students in this school limited.

ACADEMIE DES CHAMPS ELYSEES.

30 Faubourg St. Honoré, 35 Rue Boissy d'Anglas.

Jean Paul Laurens, Hector Leroux, Henri Martin, Lobrichon
and others.

FEES.

For One Month.

Half day, ... Sixty Francs.	
Whole day, . . One hundred Francs.	
Evening classes, ... Fifty Francs.	

Special conditions for men.

Criticisms given twice a week in women's class as well as men's.

V

NATIONAL MUSEUMS.

A NY person wishing to copy in the National Museums can obtain permission at the Bureau of Administration in the upper end of the lower court of the Louvre. Those in schools can obtain certificates of their masters as mentioned below. Those not in schools or studios will find either the presentation of a passport or a letter from the American Consul sufficient.

RULES CONCERNING ADMISSION OF ARTISTS AND THE PUBLIC TO THE GALLERIES.

ARTICLE I.

The Galleries of the National Museums will be opened every day except Mondays.

ARTICLE II.

No person is allowed to work in the Galleries of the National Museums without having previously obtained either a Card of Study (carte d'étude), or a special permission.

ARTICLE III.

The Cards of Study are delivered at the office of the Director every Tuesday and Thursday from 10 until 2 o'clock.

1st. To artists whose works are in these Galleries, on their personal demand.

2d. To students of the School of Fine Arts on a certificate from the Professors or Directors of the Schools.

3d. To the students in the Public Drawing Schools on demand of the Directors of the Schools, and to the students in private schools on a certificate from a master who has obtained at least one medal in the annual exhibitions.

4th. To students presented by an artist who has obtained an official medal of Paris.

5th. Temporary permissions can be accorded by the Director on verbal or written demand.

ARTICLE IV.

The public and artists will be admitted to the Galleries and Halls between 9 A. M. and 5 P. M. from April 1st to September 30th, and between 10 A. M. and 4 P. M. from October 1st to March 31st.

Sundays and holidays the Museums will be open to visitors from 10 A. M. to 4 P. M.

ARTICLE V.

All persons provided with cards must on demand show them to any agent of the National Museums who may require it.

ARTICLE VI.

All Cards of Study found in the hands of other persons than those to whom they were delivered will be suppressed immediately.

ARTICLE VII.

A general renewal of all the Cards of Study will be required every two years.

ARTICLE VIII.

The displacement of any picture exhibited in the Galleries will not be allowed under any pretext whatever.

ARTICLE IX.

THE LOUVRE.

1st. The pictures placed in the *Salon Carré* may be copied by but one person at a time; two only may copy those pictures found in the halls called the *Sept Cheminées* and the *Sept Mètres*: three will be permitted to copy the pictures placed in the other halls. All applications for copying must be registered at the office of the administration and a certificate obtained.

Three days before a copy in course of execution is to be finished, the next applicant will be notified of the arrival of his turn. If in three days after its completion, he has not presented himself, he loses his turn, and is placed at the end of the list of applicants. Two persons whose inscription numbers follow one another may arrange between themselves to alternate their working days. No person who has begun a copy may leave it for more than five days without losing his turn and passing to the last place.

The Director reserves the right of removing any copyist who, for any other excuse than illness, requires more than a reasonable time for making his copy.

2d. Those persons who wish to paint interior views of the galleries, architectural motives and ornaments, or to copy the ceilings, should send a written request to the Director.

3d. No object of art exhibited in a glass case may be withdrawn for study without permission : this having been obtained, the designated object may be placed in a particular room, called the *Salle d'Etude*.

Article X.

No copy may be removed from the Museum without a permit delivered by the head clerk or his agent. This permit must be delivered to the doorkeeper (concierge), or to an officer charged with this service.

Article XI.

The copyists must provide themselves with a piece of enamel cloth, at least one metre square, for a floor cloth.

ARTICLE XII.

Eating in the galleries is expressly forbidden. All work unconnected with the Fine Arts is also interdicted.

ARTICLE XIII.

Persons furnished with cards for study are not expected to pay for the services of the custodian, cloak room, nor for the use of the easels, stools, etc.

ARTICLE XIV.

Those who think they have cause to complain of the custodians should address themselves to the Director.

ARTICLE XV.

Order and silence must be observed in the galleries ; all persons who break this rule will be deprived of their cards.

REGULATIONS CONCERNING COPYING THE PICTURES AND STATUES IN THE LUXEMBOURG.

As the new Luxembourg Museum is not, like the old one, composed of long galleries, but of small rooms, where the view of the pictures is too often obstructed by the copyists, the Administration, in the interest of the public, is obliged to establish a new regulation.

ARTICLE I.

The Museum will be open to the copyists during the summer from 9 A. M. until 2 P. M.; during the winter from 10 A. M. to 2 P. M., Sundays and Mondays excepted.

ARTICLE II.

Several artists will not be allowed to work simultaneously before the same picture. Copyists will be admitted one by one, according to the order of their application.

ARTICLE III.

No copyist may put his name down for more than two pictures at one time.

ARTICLE IV.

Artists must complete their copies within four months, that those following may not be retarded.

VI.

SOME GENERAL INFORMATION.

THE picture shops of Paris are as a rule not so easy of entrance for students as those in this country, and dealers always keep their best pictures very carefully secluded. The student therefore must depend on the Luxembourg, the Salon, and occasional exhibitions for his acquaintance with Modern Art. At the Gallery of M. Georges Petit, in the Rue de Séze, several exhibitions are held during the year, and they are always interesting. Two Artists' Clubs, one in the Rue Volney, the other in the Place Vendome, have yearly exhibitions in the winter, at which future Salon pictures are frequently seen. Tickets for these exhibitions can usually be obtained at the studios, many of the prominent artists of Paris being members.

An American gentleman, Mr. Stewart, residing in the Avenue de Jena, has a fine collection of pictures, especially rich in the works of Fortuny, and permission to visit it is frequently given to those asking the privilege.

Occasional Exhibitions.

Galleries.

Collection of Mr. Stewart.

Churches. Some of the churches of Paris contain beautiful pictures and frescoes. Notable among them is the Pantheon, now used as a national monument and burial place. Its walls are decorated by some of the greatest living painters. The Churches of St. Vincent de Paul and St. Germain des Prés contain wonderful frescoes by Flandrin. The Church of St. Eustache has behind the altar a fine painting by Couture. Among the older churches, interesting for their history and architecture, are Notre Dame, St. Chapelle, St. Gervaix, St. Leu, St. Severin, and St. Nicolas des Champs.

The Pompeian House in the Avenue Montaigne is especially interesting to decorators. The Trocadéro has a good Museum of Architecture, and the Beaux Arts a fine collection of casts. The Fountain by Jean Goujon in the Place des Innocents, near the Marché aux Halles, is one of the most beautiful objects in Paris.

Restaurants. Among the Restaurants suitable for women are all the *Duval* Restaurants ; *Bouillon Continental,* Rue St. Honoré, near Rue St. Roch ; *Tavernier* inside Palais Royal ; *Restaurant Rue Montmartre,* opposite Passage des Panoramas ; *Maison Bourgade,* Avenue des Ternes, opposite Rue Poncelet.

Studios. Studios are likely to be found in the Rue de Douai, Rue des Martyres, Boulevard Clichy, Danton Court, Rue de Navarin, in the Clichy quarter ; Rue Bayen, off the Avenue des Ternes ; Rue Notre Dame des Champs, Rue des Saints Pères, Rue de Lille, on the left bank of the Seine.

HOTELS AND PENSIONS.

Madame Clerc, 5 Rue Ravignan. Very cheap.   **Montmartres.**

Madame Guiard, 7 Rue Brumel near Avenue de la Grande Armée. 5 francs a day.   **Porte Maillot.**

Madame Dinice, 69 bis Boulevard de Courcelles, 200 to 220 francs a month.   **Place des Ternes.**

Mlle Anarron, 40 Rue Copernic, 8 to 10 francs a day. *Miss Finlayson*, English   **Arc de Triomphe.**
Pension, 7 Rue Galilée, prices moderate. *Pension*, 18 Rue Chateaubriand, also moderate. *Pension*, 5 Rue Lord Byron, 10 francs a day.

Madame Tissier, 29 Boulevard des Batignolles, moderate.   **Clichy.**

Hotel Tête, 9 Cité du Retiro, good but expensive. *Madame Durand*, 3 Cité du Retiro, cheaper.   **Faubourg St. Honore.**

Hotel Oxford and Cambridge, 13 Rue d'Alger, corner of Rue St. Honoré. Pen-   **Vicinity of the Louvre.**
sion in this hotel can be obtained from 7 to 10 francs a day; rooms only from 2 to 3 francs. *Hotel de l'Univers et du Portugal*, 10 Rue Croix des Petits Champs. Rooms at 30 francs a month. *Hotel Prince Albert and Gibraltar*, Rue St. Hyacinthe, near Rue St. Honoré, very moderate.

Hotel Dijon and *Hotel Louis Le Grand*, both in Rue Caumartin, are spoken of as   **Conveniently near Julien's.**
moderate in their charges. *Pension, Mlle Chapuis*, 30 Rue Drouot, good but expensive, 10 to 15 francs a day.

Hotel d'Angleterre, 23 Rue Jacob, near Rue Bonaparte. *Pension, Madame Rouvier*, 6 Rue de la Sorbonne, near the Luxembourg *Hotel Voltaire*, Quai Voltaire, near Pont des Saints Pères. Rooms 3 francs a day. *Madame Estervard*, 12 Rue Littre.

COLOR MERCHANTS.

Blanchet Frères, 32 Rue Bonaparte.
Alfred Bargue fils, 33 Rue Bonaparte.
Chabod, 20 Rue Jacob.
Colin, 19 Rue des Prètres St. Germain l'Auxerrois, Place du Louvre.
Hardy-Alan, 56 Rue du Cherche-Midi.
Poulin (very cheap, but being somewhat inaccessible it is best to send an order by postal after having obtained the Catalogue). 102 Rue Turenne.
Prevost, 3 Quai Voltaire, near Pont des Saint Pères.

At nearly all the studios, merchants make semi-weekly and sometimes daily visits.

DOCTORS RECOMMENDED.

Physicians. Dr. MacGavin (allopathic), 4 St. Phillipe du Roule.

Dr. Clément (homeopathic), 62 Rue de Provence. Office hours 2 to 4.

Dentists. Drs. Bogue, Cook, and Davenport, 39 Boulevard Haussmann.

MUNICH.

Although Munich does not exert so powerful an influence in the world of art as Paris, we add the following short account of an art student's opportunities, and the expense of living in the centre of German art. The facts have been very kindly contributed by two artists who have recently resided there.

Munich has one important Art School, the Royal Academy of Fine Arts. There is an Industrial **Royal Academy** Art School, which is also a training school **of Fine Arts.** for the Academy, but that has no interest for the American student who has received the thorough training now possible in the schools at home.

The Director of the Royal Academy is (1887) Fritz Auguste Kaulbach, a young painter of the new school of German Art, distinguished for strength and truth combined with decorative quality in portraits and historic compositions.

The other professors held in highest esteem are Loefftz, Dietz and Defregger, particularly the first two.

In addition to the instruction in the life classes, there are lectures on Anatomy, Perspective, Costume, Aesthetics and kindred subjects open to the student.

The standard of proficiency required for admission is very high, because the new building of the Academy is very much crowded by students drawn thither by the popularity of the instructors.

The school year is divided into two terms, viz : from the first of October until Easter, and from Easter until the middle of July.

The fee for a foreigner is $15.00 for a half year.

The school day commences at 8 A. M., and the models pose until 12 M.

In the afternoon models are not furnished by the direction (as a rule), but can be used when paid for by the students.

Ordinary models are paid about 12 cents an hour, when sitting for the head, and 15 cents when posed for the nude. Particularly fine models command higher rates.

There is a general, but mistaken idea in America, as to the characteristics of the existing school of

The Munich Style.

painting in Munich. It is commonly supposed to be represented by the brilliant company of Americans who painted there more than ten years ago. It is not universally known that these painters were in their day, seceders from the Academy and its traditions, going apart to set up a school for themselves and calling themselves Impressionists. The tendency most noticeable in German Art to-day, is a movement following somewhat on the lines of the best old Dutch masters.

The attempt to gain richness by painting in semi-transparent bituminous tones, designedly warmer than nature, has given place to a strict search for a higher realism, a recognition of the gray quality of all light, air and space.

Though modified by the proclivities of individual masters, the general aspiration of the school is in the direction of simple external truth.

All that has been previously said in regard to the importance of cultivating the acquaintance of native painters and students is equally true here. Artistic society is more accessible in the German Art centres, Munich, Düsseldorf, Dresden, etc., because they are small towns, where all are gathered within easy calling distance about one common point of interest, the Academy of the town ; instead, as in Paris, of being diffused throughout a vast metropolis and divided in interest and allegiance between many different schools.

Artists' Society.

The customary way of living is to rent a furnished lodging, have coffee and rolls served in the room in the morning, and lunch and dine at restaurants. A comfortable bedroom can be rented from $5.00 (15 marks) a month, and upwards. Fire and lights are extra. A gratuity of 50 cents a month should be given to the servant. A good studio rents from $3.00 to $6.00 a month. Coffee with cream and rolls in the morning costs from 5 to 7 cents a day. The midday lunch, consisting of soup, roast, vegetables and dessert, costs from 20 to 25 cents a day. The same food costs a few cents more at the dinner in the evening, perhaps to cover the extra expense of lighting. A good table d'hôte dinner of soup, three courses and dessert can be had, however, for 25 cents. In the country villages, where the student would go in summer for the sketching,

Cost of Living.

furnished rooms can be rented for $4.00 a month, or less. Food is a little dearer in the country than in the town. An American can live with comfort, attend the Academy, enjoy some small luxuries, and go occasionally to the theatre and concerts for $30.00 a month.

If he has no friends in Munich, the American should go at
American Artists' Club.   once to the American Artists' Club in the Gasthaus-zur-Bluethe, Bluethe Strasse, where he will find compatriots, who will take him to see the professors, who do not speak English, and in every way aid in his establishment.

Munich is sixteen hundred and ninety feet above the sea,
Climate.   and near the Bavarian Alps. The climate is raw and changeable ; the winter wet and cold. The changes of temperature are as frequent as those of Boston but less in degree.

www.ingramcontent.com/pod-product-compliance
Lightning Source LLC
Chambersburg PA
CBHW021643270326
41931CB00008B/1144